one little thing

health transformation for the
tortoise and the hare

one
little
thing

vol. 2

StaciJoy

one little thing: health transformation for the
tortoise and the hare

Printed in the United States of America. First printing 2016

Cover and interior design: Vanessa Perez

ISBN 978-0-9851140-1-5

The theories and recommendations presented in this book are
expressed as the authors' opinions and as such are not meant to
be used to diagnose, prescribe, or to administer in any manner
to any physical ailments. In any matters related to your health,
please contact a qualified, licensed Health Practitioner.

For permission requests, write the publisher at the address
below or the email address. Requests for quantity discounts
and speaking engagement should be made via email to
JMRDistributionPublishing@gmail.com

JMR Distribution Publishing
1501 India St #103-96
San Diego, CA 92101
(916) 765-7044

CHAPTER ONE

**If you can change
a thought, you can
change your life**

We tend to live life in a hurry. Kids need to get to practice on time, making a living today takes most of our waking hours, and there never seems to be enough hours in a day to get stuff done. Whether you want to reverse a chronic disease, lower your Body Mass Index (BMI), or recover better and faster after running, this book is for you. You deserve to live the quality of life that you are willing to work for. Peace and love are not just for hippies. A thin physique is not limited to those who stop eating. To live happy and healthy is your birthright as a human being. Let your inner GPS get your there.

This book is about how to make BIG changes easily. You may be overworked and stretched like a rubber band. One more thing on your plate just might snap you in two. You need simple. You need easy. You need health. You need happiness. You need **one little thing.**

First, what is your goal?

Your destination is just ahead to the right. The anticipation of arriving at your favorite place once again is keeping you from focusing on anything else. Wait for it. A peaceful feeling comes over you as you jump off your life in the fast lane lifestyle. You love yourself and your body so much that you keep your healthy cells all jacked up on plant nutrients and you maintain a flat belly. Your bountiful energy and strong body sweep you off your feet. As you dance through life, you radiate confidence and loving kindness toward others. You've found peace within your unwavering higher power, and you are deep in the lives of your very favorite people on earth. You have arrived at this place once again, and nothing else matters. As the sun sets and the sky turns purple, you sit quietly with you. And just breathe.

I'll see it when I believe it.

How far away from this picture perfect euphoria is your life? Is there anything about what you just read that makes you think that you can't have it all? You CAN have it all. Well, at least most of it. There is good news and bad news. I always like hearing the bad news first.

BAD NEWS ALERT: We have become a sleepy nation. We have fallen asleep behind the big wheel of life. We have shut our blind eyes for too long and now we are dreaming. You cannot see what is real when you are dreaming.

GOOD NEWS ALERT: Your inner GPS Navigational System is there for you to use 24/7. You can go anywhere you desire, when you desire, and with whom you desire. It's all about perception. You have found a tool that just might get you to take that next dreaded step, only to find out that it wasn't as dreadful as you thought.

Focus your attention on what you want to see more of.

Happiness is an inside job. You can create it from within you. If someone, something, or somewhere can make you happy, they can also make you miserable. You have already given these things great power just by attaching them to an emotion like happiness. Happiness must remain an inside job because life can feel like a series of collisions along the highway. The safety belt that you wear throughout life, called inner peace or natural happiness, just might keep you alive one day when you experience a crisis in the fast lane.

Let's go road trippin' on the information super highway.

Autoimmune disorders have reached an all-time high in this country (American College of Rheumatology, 2004). School-aged children now have autoimmune disorders, such as rheumatoid arthritis, Type II diabetes, and inflammatory bowel disorders (IBD). Just a few generations ago, only the elderly population had them. Are you worried? We all should be.

Six million Americans suffer with fibromyalgia and up to 65% of these cases can co-occur with other rheumatic conditions such as rheumatoid arthritis, systemic lupus erythematosus, and ankylosing spondylitis (Center for Disease Control, 2009).

Inflammatory Bowel Disease (IBD) is a broad term that describes conditions with chronic or recurring immune response and inflammation of the gastrointestinal tract. IBD is one of the most prevalent gastrointestinal disease burdens in the United States, with an overall health care cost of more than $1.7 billion. Approximately 1.4 million Americans currently have Crohn's disease or ulcerative colitis. As many as 70,000 new cases of IBD are diagnosed in the United States each year.[1, 2]

Humans are supposed to be adaptable. Unfortunately, we have been adapting in the reverse direction for decades. I like to call this "Reverse Adaptation." Instead of getting stronger with new age technology, our current high-tech food supply and other revolutionary advancements have made us sicker, fatter, and weaker. Healthcare costs are nearly 18% of our GNP. Are you okay with this?

"Your life does not get better by chance...it gets better by change." —Jim Rohn

This is a book about why and how to change ***one little thing*** at a time. You will find recommendations of what to change within the platforms of movement, attitude, and nutrition, but the "what" is not as important as the "why" and the "how." Substitute my recommendations for your own habits. It doesn't matter what small change you make to start the change process. I care that you have a BIG reason for starting. You only need to focus on ***one little thing*** at a time. I care that you have a system in place for succeeding. I care that you are your own champion for a better life so you can feel good enough to get out there and make our world a better place. We are all speeding down the same super highway of life. You are not alone.

"You must be the change you want to see in the world." —Mahatma Gandhi

Change is easier than you think, but first you need to condition your brain to accept the change process. Your mind will do anything to keep you exactly where you have always been. In order for change to be imminent, you will need to clear your GPS history.

TRY THIS:

A simple step to learn that change is easy.

Hold an image in your mind of several things in your life that you are sincerely grateful for such as a child, a pet, a dreamy vacation home, or a special friend. Practice retrieving one or more of these images over and over again in your mind as you learn to use them to rebuild your thought patterns.

Every time a negative thought pops into your mind, immediately replace it with the warm images for which you are grateful. You may want to wear a rubber band on your wrist for a little while and snap it every time you need to make the adjustment. This will awaken your brain out of its sleepy negative patterns.

The first day, you may find that you snap and reset your mind every thirty minutes. The second day might be just as overwhelming. However, you may find the third and fourth days easier and more pleasant. Try this for one week and see how it goes. You will convince your brain that change is easy. After all, life is all about perception. Good luck and try to have fun with this.

Is your life a mess for no apparent reason?

Leo was born thirty two years ago to young parents struggling to make ends meet. He grew up in a home that considered money evil. He learned that only thieves and dirty businessmen have a lot of money. Because of the constant financial stress in the home, Leo and his four siblings experienced fighting between their parents.

Today Leo works for the state, doing a job that is neither stimulating nor satisfying to him. He dates often, but cannot seem to find the right person with whom to settle down. He finds himself living from one paycheck to the next, and often wonders if there is a better life out there. Leo has tried to lose twenty pounds over and over again but cannot seem to keep the weight off after he loses it. His health is beginning to deteriorate, and he is heading into the land of heart disease and insulin resistance. He is afraid that he will have to live this way forever: sick, lonely and poor.

Leo was negatively programmed by his family from the day he was born. He learned that money is evil. He learned that disrespecting those you care about is normal. He was conditioned to think this way. To be happy, Leo will have to change his deep programming and become a more positive thinker. Once he does this, his life will improve with less effort.

Does Leo's story feel familiar?

Traveling the road trip toward change takes time, but can lead to the life you long to live. Accept that you will lose your way from time to time. This is normal. Think of your good health as your destination.

"Check Engine" warning light

Along the way, your "Check Engine" light may illuminate as a warning that something is wrong with you. Are you feeling pain? Has your doctor diagnosed you with a disorder? Are you more than twenty percent over your normal body weight? Are you experiencing negative symptoms?

When your "Check Engine" light comes on, the most common reaction today is for you and your practitioner to smash the light off by attacking the symptoms instead of healing the root cause. Doctors often prescribe life-long pharmaceutical and over-the-counter drugs, administer chemotherapy, or surgically remove affected body parts to get that "Check Engine" light off. But they don't lift up the hood and fix deeper breakdown in your body.

"Houston, we have a problem!"

YOU FORGOT TO CHECK UNDER THE HOOD

What do you do when the "Check Engine" light comes on in your car? You have a mechanic find the problem in the engine and fix it, right? Conventional western medicine often fails to check the engine when the "Check Engine" light of serious medical symptoms becomes illuminated. When you experience serious medical symptoms, you usually need to rebuild your engine (repairing your gut will overhaul your immune system) and change your filter (detoxify the liver). Stop smashing out your warning light by only treating symptoms of a bigger problem. Instead, if you become proficient at overhauling and maintaining both your gut engine and your liver filter, there is a higher probability that your "Check Engine" light will no longer be a problem and you will continue life's journey with a healthy body.

My life changed forever when I bought a car with a built in GPS navigational system. It gave me peace of mind that I was going to get to my programmed destination no matter how many U-turns or wrong turns I made. I now feel safe on the road and I know where I'm going.

The GPS does not care where you have been.

The only thing your GPS cares about is getting you from where you are at this exact moment to where you told it you want to go. There is only one thing you can do when you feel yourself deviating off of your route.

RECALCULATE ROUTE!

This is the most important phrase you can add to your health vocabulary. It allows you to gently readjust your path when you veer off course without making you feel like a failure. What is it about recalculating the route that can send people into a flurry of negative self-talk and feelings of inadequacy? You are simply readjusting to reach your desired goal.

RECALCULATE ROUTE and move on. It's a beautiful journey if you choose to see it that way.

The first step in any health restoration program is to figure out where you want to go.

Be realistic. You can't drive from California to New York in two days, but you can enjoy the journey along the way and arrive with a smile in ten days. Have the courage to set a destination that is achievable and avoid recalculating your route too many times. This will only confuse the mother board in your GPS. Once you've decided where you want to go, just take it slowly and enjoy the spectacular views and side stops along the way.

What is your desired outcome?

Where do you want to go?

Do you want to release 5 or more pounds?

Do you want to add more peace and balance to your life?

Do you want to live in a positive space instead of the negative zone?

Do you want more energy in the afternoon hours?

Do you want to eat more fruits and vegetables and live a plant-based life style?

Do you want to reverse a disease?

Do you want to repair a relationship?

Spend quality time choosing your goal before taking the next step, because what you write will determine everything you do from this point forward. This is where you will program your GPS to take you where you want to go.

Write your destination(s) in the space provided below:_____

_____

_____

_____

_____

_____

Believe in yourself.

Believe you can do it!

Jane came to me several years ago, exasperated by not being able to lose weight. Every "die"-t failed her over time. She repeatedly lost ten pounds then gained back fifteen until she gave up. After determining that she wanted to lose 30 pounds in order to feel sexy and connected with her partner again, we worked on raising her self-esteem and we started a journey in partnership. The first thing she did was spend the next four months becoming a water drinker again like she used to when she was in her 20's. She was asked to keep her urine clear all day. Hydrating her internal desert gave her more energy to move her body four days a week, which eventually inspired her to make different food choices. She started by adding a whole food supplement to her daily regimen, which provided her with the micro-nutrition that she needed to burn calories more efficiently. After building the supplement habit, she was ready to become a plant-based eater. Jane added a large salad, or four servings of vegetables, and two large fruits to her day. She supplemented her daily calories with two healthy, plant-based protein smoothies.

Jane added **one little thing** every month, and she dropped three dress sizes and fifteen pounds in one year. After adding hydration, regular physical activity, proper supplementation and eight more servings of produce to her life each day, she melted inches from her frame. During her change process, she worried that the number on her scale was not moving much. I reassured her that her new found lean muscle mass weighs more than her fat. Today, several years later, she is living happily while maintaining her goal weight.

What are the reasons why you desire your goals?

What emotions fuel them?

Do you want to feel more sexy and confident in a bikini?

Do you want to feel self-respect when you set a goal, work toward it and achieve it?

Do you want to feel Ohana family love as you play with your grandkids on the floor?

Do you want to feel peaceful and accomplished in the presence of your big beautiful family at your child's wedding?

Do you want to live through these family milestones?

Do you want to help raise your grandkids?

Write down your own "whys" in the space below. Think about the deep emotions behind your dreams:

Now that you are connected to your personal destination, and have a "why" for taking the actions in this book, are you ready to learn more about your **one little thing**?

"Change is never easy. You fight to hang on and you fight to let go." —The Wonder Years

Change at your own pace.

You do not have to be a superhero to make the changes that will profoundly affect your life. You can take this step-by-step and go slowly, or you can jump all in and feel the magic. Remember the *Tortoise and The Hare*? "Slow and steady wins the race" and stands the test of time, my friend. Once you figure out which character you are as you navigate through the change process, the rest of the road trip is fun and simple, but still may not be easy.

Are you the Tortoise or the Hare?

TORTOISE	HARE
You talk things out with your partner or friends	You tend to be impulsive or compulsive
It takes you a long time to change	You have a well-developed intuition
You procrastinate	You act quickly and clean up later
You tend to frustrate others	Others may not keep up with you
You try not to take on too many things	You are the lead volunteer task master
You contemplate before you act	It's fun when you jump all in
Feeling pressure tends to shut you down	You work better under pressure

When it comes to change, the Tortoise can move forward by adding **one little thing** to his life each month. The Hare may choose to jump in and take on the great transformation described at the end of this book. He can always clean up the mess later.

Your new life awaits you.

Buckle up and enjoy the ride.

CHAPTER TWO

Find your move groove

It's no mystery why one third of America is obese and another third is overweight.[3] We don't move enough. We work longer hours than ever, often sitting all day. Exhausted from a long, stressful day, we park ourselves on the couch when we get home. We feel stressed out much of the time. To calm our stress and cheer ourselves up, we eat far too many calories from fat, sugar, and chemicals. Our processed diets miss the nutrients found in plants.

MOVE and GROOVE!

More than one half of our population does not exercise at all, according to the Center for Disease Control and

Prevention.[4] Obesity is putting us at risk for cancer, heart disease, and other unpleasant, high-risk, expensive disorders.

Move it, use it or lose it.

Your heart needs some exercise to survive. Heart disease is the leading cause of death for both men and women in America. About 610,000 people die of heart disease in the United States every year. That's one in every four deaths.[5] Coronary heart disease (CHD) is the most common type of heart disease, killing over 370,000 people annually.[5]

More than a third of heart attacks can be avoided by regular aerobic activity, yet only a third of Americans exercise regularly.[6]

Just a simple stretch

Stretching is an easy activity that can change your life. No matter what your athletic level is, it's easy to stretch. You don't have to spend much time doing it to have huge results! Here are just a few of the benefits you can expect from a regular stretching program:

- **Feel less muscle stress**
- **Increase your reach and flexibility**
- **Relieve muscle pain**
- **Become more agile and athletic**
- **Bring more oxygen to your body, making you healthier**
- **Experience fewer back problems**
- **Avoid injuries**
- **Have more energy**
- **Feel more alive**

TRY THIS:
JUST STRETCH

Create a stretching routine that feels comfortable, and stretch every day at the same time for thirty days. If you are feeling unsafe or insecure, consider hiring a personal fitness professional who can help you jumpstart into a safe, fun routine.

Begin with a gentle, easy set of stretches then advance into more complex moves. Don't bounce, but do hold the stretch for at least 20 seconds. Don't do anything that hurts. Stretch with a buddy.

More complex strategy: Start a yoga or Pilates routine. Be prepared to change your life!

Just move.

Regardless of age, weight or athletic ability, aerobic activity or cardiovascular exercise is good for you. As your body adapts to regular aerobic exercise, you'll get stronger and feel more in control.

Here are just a few benefits that you can expect when maintaining a cardio routine:

- **Strengthen your heart**
- **Reduce health problems**
- **Help manage chronic conditions**
- **Keep your arteries clear**
- **Feel happier**
- **Increase stamina and energy**
- **Live longer**
- **Get sick less often**

Any movement helps you.

If you don't exercise at all, start with something simple like a walk around the block. Choose an activity that feels easy. Don't psyche yourself into thinking you have to do something complicated, like go on a long run or join a gym. Don't worry if your action feels silly and small. The idea is to get moving.

Put your life in forward motion. Light your pilot light. Congratulate yourself on your effort and allow yourself to become inspired that you have gotten into action. Find an exercise buddy. Create your own personal cheerleaders within your partner, your spouse, your children, or your friends. When others support you, you may hold yourself more accountable to the commitment that you've made to yourself because the world is watching your every step. The social pressure actually helps you in the long run.

Some of you are at a more advanced level and will choose a more sophisticated ***one little thing*** that supports where you are at the moment. Is your ***one little thing*** running three miles every day or spending two hours in the gym five days a week? You will know what you need. Follow your instincts, choose the appropriate activity for YOU and apply the ***one little thing*** principles as you go.

TRY THIS
JUST WALK

It seems so simple, doesn't it? Add WALKING to your daily routine. Go out and buy new sneakers, if you must. Look good in your exercise outfit, if that matters to you. The preliminary steps are not important. Just WALK. Put one foot in front of the other and walk from Point A to Point B.

If you are especially new to walking as exercise, buy a Fitbit or get a step counter app for your phone. Add 2,000 steps to your week at first. You can raise the bar to 10,000 steps later. It doesn't matter if you walk slowly or briskly. It doesn't matter if you walk the dog, walk the stroller, or walk the treadmill. Just WALK. The idea is to simply get moving. You may become so good at walking, that you will want to walk routinely for the rest of your life.

Try this for 30 days.

Make regular entries in your calendar to walk for ten minutes four days every week and honor those times. Come on now, you can do anything for 30 days. Just get moving. You don't need to change ANYTHING else. If you want to add something else to your regimen, go ahead. This is YOUR road trip. YOU have the GPS all set!

Make it fun! Sing with the music. Breathe. Wear outfits that don't match. Take a buddy. Walk in nature or a park. Make it count.

Park far away from the building and WALK. But use your judgment and be safe. Don't park far away from the building if you know that you will have to walk back to your car alone at night. Be sensible and be smart.

Forget about the elevator or the escalator. Take the stairs. Every step counts!

This **one little thing** might seem stupid and simple, but trust the process. Do it for 30 days and see how you feel. Then, you can choose another **one little thing**...or NOT. The choice is yours to make, every step of the way.

As always, if you have health issues, such as heart disease or structural difficulties with your spine or joints, make sure that you discuss a plan with your medical practitioner to add more walking to your life. Please be safe and be sensible.

Strengthen your core.

Core work is different from strength-training programs that isolate a single muscle group. Instead, they challenge as many muscles as possible in integrated, coordinated movements. Core moves should engage your entire body, from head to toe. They strengthen your center and help your body work together as a unit. Yoga and Pilates are great for working your core because the postures target those muscle groups.

Here are just a few benefits that you can expect when maintaining a core routine:

- **Alleviate back pain**
- **Improve posture**
- **Improve athletic performance**
- **Better balance**

There are countless other activities to strengthen your core, from swimming to cycling to kick boxing. Talk to your trainer or exercise specialist about a routine that's right for you. It may be helpful to have an expert show you how to do some moves with proper form, so you can do them safely and effectively on your own.

TRY THIS:

Add push-ups and planks

Here's a simple way to strengthen the core of your body. Add 20 PUSH-UPS and a ONE-MINUTE PLANK to your day, every day. It doesn't matter if you do straight-legged push-ups or knees-on-the-floor push-ups. The simple routine will add lean muscle mass to your arms and core muscle group. Then, if you fall one day, your upper body will not be so weak that you won't be able to get up again. None of us wants to be helpless on the ground, crying, "I've fallen and I can't get up! Where is my emergency button necklace?"

If you can't do twenty push-ups, do them until you literally cannot do one more, and try again the next day. You'll eventually be able to do 20 push-ups. Practice the bent-arm plank every day until you can hold the position for one full minute.

This is what a plank looks like: Make your body straight and stiff as a wooden plank. The only two things that should be touching the floor are your bent toes and your forearms at a 90-degree angle. Look down at the floor and loosen your neck muscles. Pull in and tighten your abdominal muscles. Remember to breathe. Hold that pose for one full minute. It's simple, but it's not easy.

Practice both of these exercises for the rest of your life and your body will change over time.

Maintaining regular movement is a challenge for many people. Acknowledge this and be kind to yourself. If you get busy and neglect your movement for a day, a week or a month, then just begin again. Don't beat yourself up or think that a wrong turn means you're hopelessly lost. RECALCULATE ROUTE is always an option for you if you take the leap forward, then swerve off course. Be proud of yourself for setting the goal to take your body back.

CHAPTER THREE

Visualize Whirled Peas

ATTITUDE

When Lisa turned 40, she decided to gain more control of her health. She had been experiencing chronic pain all over her body, trouble sleeping, and a foggy brain for several years. Her symptoms had worsened as time passed, but she ignored them, hoping that they would disappear on their own.

Lisa consulted her doctor, who ordered a battery of tests. When the bloodwork came back normal, he told her that her symptoms were all in her head. He handed her a prescription for an anti-anxiety medication, a referral to a psychiatrist, and walked her to the exit door with a hand shake and a sympathetic look. Lisa didn't fill the prescription or call the psychiatrist.

She did not buy his diagnosis of anxiety. Her doctor's response was the only thing that gave her anxiety. Lisa was in constant pain and exhausted from lack of sleep. Getting nowhere with her doctor, she went in search of a second opinion.

After two visits with a new doctor recommended by a friend, and more blood tests, Lisa was given a diagnosis of exacerbation of fibromyalgia. Her new doctor felt fairly confident in his diagnosis. Unfortunately, he did not have many ideas on how to treat her disorder. He told Lisa to clean up her diet and manage her stress, then return in three weeks.

Lisa felt alone in an uncertain world. She was desperate to feel better. That is when she met me. From the start we both knew that this new road would lead her to her healing. I gave Lisa two options. She could take the Hare path and overhaul her life with a strict detoxification program.

Or she could follow the Tortoise method and start the **one little thing** program at a slower, less intense pace. She chose simple and slow.

The first thing that Lisa chose to add to her life was better thoughts. She agreed to live each day intentionally, focusing on gratitude, even if she was feeling frustrated, angry, exhausted, scared, or hopeless. She immediately understood the power of putting positive thoughts in her mind. She began repeating a series of affirmations that would eventually lead her in the direction of right thinking, and would lead her toward the right actions. "Thank you for my healing" and "I feel more powerful every day" topped her list of positive reprogramming messages. After raising her mental bar for 30 days, she decided to take on her nutrition.

Lisa was unaware of how nutrition affected her health. We went to work on nutrition theory, such as why and how to keep her body alkaline, how to keep her inflammation down, and how phytonutrients in whole foods positively affect her health. She learned the consequences associated with ingesting harmful pesticides and chemicals, aspartame and other sweeteners, and hard to pronounce preservatives that depleted her health.

Lisa was a dream client, open to the information, and understanding concepts quickly. She decided to take her nutrition to the next level by adding whole food concentrates in capsules with double doses consistently for four months. She combined capsules with two vegan protein shakes every day, using a milk alternative base, loaded up with green leafy vegetables, ground flax seeds, and soaked chia seeds.

After four months, Lisa noticed that she craved more fruits and vegetables. She started eating more salads and naturally increased her water intake by nearly 50 percent. Eight months had passed since we began working together. Lisa noticed a decrease in the intensity of her body aches from an "8" down to "4" on her worst days. She reported feeling better-rested. Her brain fog was lifting. Although she was moving in the right direction, she knew she had not yet reached her final destination. There was more work to do.

Lisa was ready for deeper healing. I suggested a meditation program to clear her mind and to reach a higher spiritual awareness. After reading *The Relaxation Response*, she began a four-month climb toward a higher perspective. Lisa meditated for five minutes a day, which soon turned into ten minutes, and eventually became thirty minutes. She found a spiritual guide, who gently pointed her in the right direction, helping her process to unfold. After only four weeks of consistent mind clearing meditation, Lisa began crying during her meditations. Without knowing why she felt so sad, her spiritual teacher suggested that she lean into her tears while listening to her inner voice, or God's whispers.

Eventually, Lisa became more aware of her grief. Her emotions continued to lead her quiet mind back to her failed marriage nearly ten years prior. She pushed down her emotional responses to the divorce. Her friends and family kept telling her to be strong and to carry on, so she did. But she still had repressed grief. This new found clarity lifted a 100 ton weight off of her psyche. She was becoming liberated from the vice grip that her subconscious suffering had over her. Lisa's next series of actions involved clearing her emotional pain with Emotional Freedom Technique (EFT), loving herself and accepting herself in the present, forgiving herself for everything, and apologizing for her part in the break up with her ex-husband in a conversation with him. They remain good friends to this day.

Lisa used the **one little thing** program to heal her life. She is currently thriving in a new marriage with a partner who understands her and supports her in every way. She is living a pain free, positive lifestyle. She practices vegetarianism, yoga, and higher love.

Your mind is a terrible thing to waste.

Our thoughts can make us strong or make us weak. When Lisa changed the way she was thinking while quieting her mind, her life finally moved in the direction she wanted.

Maharishi Mahesh Yogi (1918–2008) was a spiritual teacher who started the Transcendental Meditation movement in the United States. In the late 1960s and early 1970s, the Maharishi achieved fame as the guru to the Beatles and other celebrities. He introduced the world to the power of quieting the mind.

Calm your mind and reduce your stress.

In 1975, Herbert Benson M.D., an Associate Professor of Medicine at the Harvard Medical School and Director of the Hypertension Department of Boston's Beth Israel Hospital, moved the practice of meditation deeper into the Western world when he published a book called *The Relaxation Response*.[7] He reached an entire missed segment of the population that shuts down to the benefits of meditation because it can be hard for westerners to relate to TM language. Dr. Benson approached the topic from a place of stress reduction. He explained what happens to us when we experience stress, and how quieting our mind and body changes us all the way down to the cell.

Here are just a few of the benefits of regular relaxation and meditation:

- **Reduce oxygen consumption to give you more energy**
- **Decrease blood pressure**
- **Decrease respiratory rate**
- **Decrease heart rate**
- **Decrease muscle tension**
- **Decrease stress**
- **Think more clearly**

The purpose of meditation is to make our mind calm and peaceful. If our mind is peaceful, we will be free from worries and mental discomfort, and we will experience true happiness; but if our mind is not peaceful, we will find it very difficult to be happy, even if we are living in the very best conditions.

Usually, we find it difficult to control our minds. It seems as if our minds are like a balloon in the wind, blown here and there by external circumstances. If things go well, our minds are happy, but if bad things happen, we immediately become unhappy. Such fluctuations of mood arise because we are too closely attached to the external situation. We are like children making a sandcastle: excited at first, but upset when the incoming tide destroys our creation.

By training in meditation, we create an inner space and clarity that enables us to control our minds regardless of the external circumstances. Gradually we develop a mental balance that is happy all the time, rather than an unbalanced mind that oscillates between the extremes of excitement and despair. It is in this space of liberation that we can experience mostly peace and happiness.

TRY THIS:

A simple breathing meditation

The first stage of meditation is to stop distractions and make your mind clearer and more lucid. You can do this with a simple breathing meditation.

Choose a quiet place to meditate and sit in a comfortable position. You can sit in the traditional cross-legged posture or in any other comfortable position. You even can sit in a chair, if that works better. Just keep your back straight to prevent your mind from becoming sluggish or sleepy.

Sit with your eyes partially closed. Turn your attention to your breathing. Breathe naturally, preferably through your nostrils, without attempting to control your breath. Try to become aware of the sensation of the breath as it enters and leaves your nostrils. This sensation is the focus of your meditation. Try to concentrate on it to the exclusion of everything else in your body or around you.

At first, your mind will be very busy with thoughts. You might even feel that the meditation makes your mind busier. In reality, you are just becoming more aware of how busy your mind actually is. There will be a great temptation to follow different thoughts as they arise, but you should resist this and remain focused on the sensation of the breath. If you notice that your mind has wandered and is following your thoughts, immediately return your focus to your breathing. Repeat this as many times as necessary until your mind stays on your breath.

Your mind is a powerful thing.

When you fill it with positive thoughts, your life will change.

If you practice patiently in this way, gradually your distracting thoughts will subside and you will experience a sense of inner peace and relaxation. Your mind will feel spacious and refreshed. When the sea is rough, sediment is churned up and the water becomes murky, but when the wind dies down the mud gradually settles and the water becomes clear. In a similar way, when the flow of your distracting thoughts is calmed through concentrating on the breath, your mind becomes unusually clear. You should stay with this state of mental calm for awhile.

Even though breathing meditation is only a preliminary stage of meditation, it can be quite powerful. This practice can show you that it is possible to experience inner peace and contentment just by controlling your mind, without having to depend at all upon external conditions. When the turbulence of distracting thoughts subsides and your mind becomes still, a deep happiness and contentment naturally arises from within you. This feeling of contentment and well-being helps you to cope with the busy-ness and difficulties of daily life. So much of the stress and tension you may normally experience comes from your mind. Many of the problems you may experience, including ill health, stem from this stress. Just by doing breathing meditation for ten or fifteen minutes each day, you can reduce this stress. You can experience a calm, spacious feeling in the mind, and many of your problems will fall away. Difficult situations will become easier to deal with. You can feel happier and more accepting of others. Then your relationships will improve.

Not only can your thoughts strengthen you, but they can also crush you. Thoughts stimulate feelings, feelings inspire action, and your actions create your character and your circumstances.

This isn't a new idea. Developing a positive mental attitude was introduced in 1937 by Napoleon Hill in the book *Think and Grow Rich*. The book never uses the term, but developed the importance of positive thinking as a principle to personal and financial success.

Your mind holds the key to your happiness. As you grow up, certain images and messages become programmed deep within the subconscious mind. You may have difficulty changing them once you learn them. These images represent your attitudes, beliefs and triggers that cause you to behave the way you do.

If you want to change your life, you must first reprogram the messages living deep within your mind. Do you feel unworthy at times? Do you feel good or bad about earning money? Do you feel pretty? Do people call you the very moment that you are thinking about them? Do you attract others or repel them? All of these things have everything to do with subconscious programming.

"No one can make you feel inferior without your consent." ~Eleanor Roosevelt

If you can accept that your mood is a choice, you may be more likely to improve your positive mental attitude. Louise Hay has built her entire career on teaching the world how to use affirmations to improve their lives. She teaches us how to reprogram the subconscious mind through daily affirmations, which eventually changes the way we view our world. This dictates the way that we act and the things that we do and say.

Change your thoughts, change your life.

TRY THIS:

Gratitude check

Put a rubber band around your wrist. For the next 30 days, whenever a bad thought or memory pops into your mental box, snap the rubber band and immediately visualize two things in your life for which you are extremely grateful. Make these things BIG, like your kids, your spouse, your family pet, your income, or your home. My gratitude check is always my three children, Joe, Marc and Rose.

Keep it simple. Bad thought...SNAP... Then, I intentionally flood my mind with visions of my beautiful kids and...BAM... the bad thought disappears. Then I float through the rest of my day feeling good about my kids.

Sleep your way to happiness!

When it comes to attitude, the most important thing is sleep. It seems so simple, but millions of people are falling asleep at the wheel of life because they don't sleep enough in their beds at night. They are tired. They're short-tempered. They're easily frustrated. They're inefficient, making frequent mistakes.

It's much more difficult to maintain a positive mental attitude with yourself and with others when you suffer from sleep deprivation and jack your adrenaline up with caffeine jolts throughout the day.

Here are just a few of the benefits of getting a full night's rest:

- **Improve memory**
- **Lengthen your attention span**
- **Stabilize mood swings**
- **Increase mental alertness**
- **Focus better**
- **Restore your health by secreting more Human Growth Hormone**
- **Heal mentally and physically**

TRY THIS:

SLEEP

Focus your attention on getting to sleep every night at an hour that will give you at least seven hours of sleep. Some people need eight hours, but if you consistently fall short in this area, start by programming a realistic destination. If you know that your eyes pop open at 5:00 am every morning, lay your head down on your pillow no later than 10:00 pm.

Try this for 30 days and you might be pleasantly surprised. This takes some discipline because there are so many things you can be doing at night, like painting your nails, catching up with work or email, cruising Facebook, doing laundry, working on that airplane model, cleaning your windows, or organizing your junk drawer. Let it go. Getting enough sleep so you are clear and calm for tomorrow is more important than emails, chores, hobbies, or social media.

Getting to bed at a reasonable hour is a sign of self-respect. Honor your nervous system. Be kind to your body. The sleep you give yourself will pay you back with more efficiency and focus throughout the next day.

Now that you have the sleep thing down, you might be ready to take on another ***one little thing***...or NOT. Remember, this journey belongs to you. You are in complete control of your destination and your efforts in getting there.

CHAPTER FOUR

Keep right at the fork

Nutrition

Our bodies run on fuel, just like cars do. Our fuel is the nutrition in our food. Giving your body healthy food helps you go further and reduces the risk of a break down. Proper nutrition also allows you to overhaul your engine and change your filter when your "Check Engine" light illuminates.

High quality fuel will both prevent and repair damage. But so many of us think of food as our source of joy. We choose foods based on a specific taste or what we are used to eating. You need to understand that processed food or food treated with harmful pesticides is junk-o fuel. It contains toxic chemicals that will take up residence in your fat cells as a way to protect your engine parts and your gastrointestinal tract from becoming corroded. The amount of fat your body hangs onto is directly related to the amount of harmful chemicals you have managed to accumulate from a toxic food supply, drinking water, cleaning agents, beauty products, and other environmental pollutants.

Your liver is your body's filter. It has a BIG job to do. It is designed to convert toxins into a form that can easily be excreted out of the body through urine. Once the toxicity is removed, your body no longer needs the fat for protection. Then it will eventually melt off your body and exit through feces.

Your liver filter needs two things to purify toxins from your body. It needs an abundant supply of raw fruits and vegetables, and it needs large amounts of clean, fresh water.

Water is your best friend.

When it comes to nutrition, the most important and logical **one little thing** to add to your life is water. We cannot live more than a few days without water.

Pure, clean, filtered water can be the difference between weight loss, weight gain, a cloudy mind and clarity, or inflammation and pain-free living.

Water hydrates every cell in your body, and it keeps your kidneys active and functional. Water moves waste materials from your bloodstream and your intestines. It keeps your brain functioning. It allows every system in your body to do what it's designed to do, which helps you reach your highest human potential. Water is life, and the purity of your water makes all the difference.

TRY THIS:

HYDRATE!

Are you getting enough water? Every time you urinate, notice the color and the odor. If it is any shade of yellow or has a strong odor, you are dehydrated. Drink one or two glasses of water immediately. The objective is to keep your urine clear. You might have trouble counting ounces of water throughout your busy day. Just keep your urine clear by drinking water all day and you won't have to worry about anything else.

Is it finally time to overhaul your engine?

Autoimmune disorders, such as thyroid disorders, celiac, rheumatoid arthritis, psoriasis, fibromyalgia, and type

2 diabetes, are on the rise in the US. There are several theories for this. "Increased intestinal permeability is observed in association with autoimmune diseases," according to an analysis published for the National Institute of Health. In other words, leaky gut leads to many of the diseases plaguing Americans in our modern era.[8]

Your gastrointestinal tract is your immune system's home base. You may need to overhaul this engine to repair your body. Toxins can irritate, then damage the wall of your intestinal tract. Some of the common substances that destroy our intestines include: gluten (a protein found in wheat, barley, rye, and some oats), various types of pharmaceutical and over-the-counter medications, acute stress, and processed foods containing genetically modified ingredients. GMOs are a combination of glyphosate, BT toxin, and other health depleting agents.[9] Just about every food consumed in the US is a GMO unless labeled "non-GMO" or "certified organic."

As these factors wreak their havoc on our digestive tract, the lining of the intestines and blood vessels become leaky or permeable. This causes foreign substances, such as protein molecules, to leak through the lining of the intestines into the abdominal space where the immune system lives. The immune army becomes overstimulated as it attempts to manage the foreign invaders nearby. As the immune system revs up to high RPMs, it turns its excess energy against you and breaks down your entire body, cell by cell, organ by organ, system by system. This may result in autoimmune disorders, life threatening food allergies, and inflammatory bowel diseases. Years of exposure to food and environmental toxins causes immune breakdown. The results devastate the health of most of our population, as well as the healthcare system that is designed to support us.

Consider rebuilding your engine and changing your filter if you suffer from any of the following conditions:

•Addison's Disease •Asthma
•Alzheimer's Disease •Celiac Disease
•Crohn's Disease •Diabetes •Eczema
•Endometriosis •Epstein Barr Virus
•Fibromyalgia •Grave's Disease
•Guillain-Barre Syndrome •Hemolytic
Anemia •Huntington's Chorea
•Interstitial •Cystitis •Irritable Bowel
Syndrome •Life Threatening Food
Allergies •Lupus •Meniere's Disease
•Mononucleosis •Multiple Sclerosis (MS)
• Myasthenia Gravis •Osteoporosis

- Parkinson's Disease •Peripheral
- Neuropathy •Pernicious Anemia
- Psoriasis •Restless Leg Syndrome
- Rheumatoid •Arthritis •Scleroderma
- Ulcerative Colitis •Urticaria (hives)

The benefits of organic farming:

- **Organic produce contains fewer harmful pesticides, meaning fewer chemicals.**
- **Organic food is often fresher.**
- **Organic farming is better for the environment.**
- **Organically raised animals are NOT given antibiotics, growth hormones, or fed animal byproducts.**
- **Organic meat and milk are richer in certain nutrients.**
- **Organic food is GMO-free.**

We all have to eat to live. Nutrition is our fuel. Unfortunately, the conversion of food into energy has a price tag, and the consequence is cellular damage, aka oxidative stress. This leads to just about every disease known to man.

Good nutrition relies on consistently eating a variety of fruits and vegetables that come from the ground, tree, vine, and sea. These foods decrease inflammation and slow the aging process by keeping your body chemistry closer to alkaline than acidic.

To grasp why you need to eat mainly fruits and vegetables, you need to understand *oxidative stress*. Once you comprehend the reason these foods are more powerful, you will feel more motivated to choose your **one little thing** to change in your nutrition...or not. It's your choice.

Your cells are under constant attack from oxidation.

When oxygen, heat and wood create energy, a fire burns. The byproduct of this oxidation is smoke and soot. These are harmful toxins, which is why many areas have limits on how often you can burn wood.

When gasoline mixes with oxygen, it produces horsepower in an engine. The byproduct of this oxidation is carbon monoxide, a poisonous gas that can bring down any human and also pollutes our air.

When an apple is cut open and the nutrients are exposed to oxygen, the apple turns brown and kids toss it in the trash in the lunchroom.

Oxidation harms your cells, too.

You can see how many things in life oxidize. Let's translate this concept to the metabolism of food. We eat food. The food passes through the gastrointestinal tract as we digest it and breaks down into useful molecules for the production of life-sustaining energy. This energy, or ATP, is produced in the mitochondrion. I like to call this structure the "battery" of the cell.

When food molecules go through the chemical process of producing energy in the mitochondria, the byproduct is an infinite number of unstable electrons called free radicals. These electrons are like sparks that seek and destroy molecules, cells, tissue, then eventually organs and entire body systems. Every cell in the body takes more than 10,000 daily hits because free radicals try to pull electrons from other atoms. Electrons are more stable when they travel in pairs, just like humans. When free radicals tear electrons away from the atoms in your cells, your cells become unstable and break down. Free radical damage to the body is called oxidative stress.

Oxidative stress is synonymous with aging, disease and eventually death. Don't let this alarm you. Oxidative stress is as natural as a ripened leaf falling off of its branch in autumn. The good news is that we can control the rate of our own oxidative process. Understanding how can empower you to make smarter choices along your journey.

Free radical electron sparks are destructive. When they hit our joint tissue, we develop arthritis inflammation, and pain. Our entire immune system is highly susceptible to free radical damage and can eventually affect allergy symptoms, colds, flus, and cancer cell growth. DNA, our genetic coding, and the blueprint for how every cell replicates, is susceptible to free radical hits, causing a cluster of abnormal cells called cancer.

As more oxygen is pumped through respiration and moves through the chemical process, higher oxidative stress and more cellular damage can occur. Athletes breathe in more oxygen and have a higher energy output. Because their bodies need more energy to fuel their heightened activity, their fireplace burns more wood at higher temperatures, increasing their oxidative stress levels.

Slowing down aging is simple.

Once you understand the concept of oxidative damage, you can work to slow it down, and your body can start repairing itself. Free radicals need an electron partner in order to become more stable in the body. We can provide electrons in the form of antioxidants (against oxidation) by eating colorful foods that come from the ground. The electrons in antioxidants pair with the free radical electrons, so the free radicals won't pull as many electrons from the atoms in our own cells.

When we eat large amounts of colorful foods of the rainbow that come from the ground, trees, vines, or the sea, their antioxidants work in synergy to donate their electrons to the volatile and destructive free radicals. This slows down oxidation and the aging process in our bodies. It is that simple: eating more produce slows your aging.

Then why is it so hard for us to do?

If we know fruits and vegetables make us healthier and slow aging, then why don't more of us eat plenty of them? Food has become our source of pleasure.

The foods we eat often have emotional connections to our childhoods or cultures. When we eat food because of habit or to feed our emotions, we ignore that it can either fuel us or slowly kill us. As part of modern human civilization, we must recognize that our food either ages us more rapidly or slows down the aging process. Rich, energy-producing, life-sustaining nutrition can fuel and heal our bodies.

Most of us have lost our connection to nutrition as we are bombarded in the endless forest of health-depleting, factory foods. Corporations, fixated on selling more cheaply-produced foods, saturate the media with processed foods filled with artificial flavor enhancers that don't give us proper nutrition.

Now that you understand the devastating toll oxidative stress takes on your body, it's time to figure out how to get more fruits and vegetable nutrients. If you don't want to start putting more produce into your diet, you have other choices for easier changes that will help you fight free radicals. There is another **one little thing** you can change...or NOT. You are in control of the ride.

Eat plants.

If you are not ready to increase the number of plant foods you eat just yet, consider the idea of making whole food concentrates part of your nutrition.

As a holistic public health nurse, I constantly search for inexpensive, and easy-to-master things that make enormous improvements in people's overall health. Supplementation is one of those things. There is a logical process to follow when choosing the right supplement.

Consider two vital criteria that are important when searching for a supplement.

The first choice is whether to eat your supplements in isolated form or whole food form. I recommend whole food supplements.

Isolated supplements are either genetically modified in a laboratory, or a specific nutrient, such an antioxidant, is pulled out of an edible substance. But an isolated nutrient is not natural and has been shown to negatively affect high-risk individuals.[10] It is similar to putting a carburetor and a cylinder together and expecting the engine to run. A nutrient usually works more powerfully in its natural form, accompanying other nutrients in food.

Whole food supplementation is different from an isolated nutrient formula because it is made from the concentrated juice powders of foods that grow in the ground. The nutrients are delivered in full synergy with the other thousands of nutrients found in the whole food.

When humans eat a supplement formula, do good things happen in the body? I look for research that proves bio-availability. In other words, does it absorb into the bloodstream? I also want to see a reduction of oxidative stress throughout the body. This is what whole foods do for us when we eat them. You want your supplement to do the same thing. I like to see that a supplement has at least three well-designed, independent studies confirming these things. Any supplement that I take or recommend must be proven safe and effective.

My favorite daily, forever supplement is *Juice Plus*+ because of the depth of a growing collection of independent research that confirms its safety and effectiveness when humans take it.[11] If research is not available for a supplement you take, you will have to hope it works based on blind faith. Blind faith is not good enough when it comes to things we put in our bodies every day. I am not willing to take any risks when it comes to my daily supplement.

If a whole food supplement sounds like something you could add to your life more easily than a complete overhaul of your diet, you can learn more and explore the research on your own. Whole food supplements can also help fortify your diet even if you are adding fresh produce. You can see the benefits for yourself. Or not. The choice is up to you.

CHAPTER FIVE

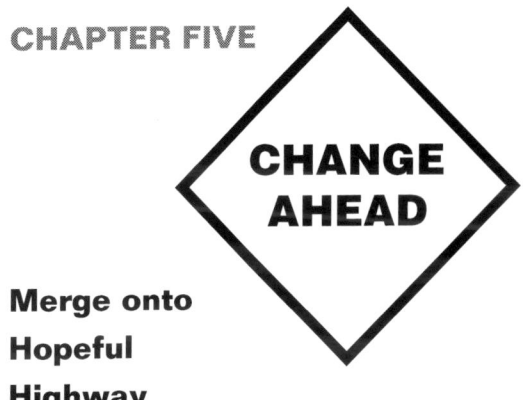

CHANGE
AHEAD

Merge onto
Hopeful
Highway

THE GREAT TRANSFORMATION

Aaron stood naked, staring into the mirror. His attention shifted onto the 55 extra pounds that glared back at him. When did this happen? Who was this man? At age 52, Aaron was living an unstable lifestyle as an award-winning chef in his community. His sleeping patterns were weakening him. He suffered with daily chest pains. He didn't move much, and he felt depressed. Though he was surrounded by food all day in his work, he ate sporadically, and was making poor food choices, filled with empty carbohydrates and fatty meat. Alcohol had become Aaron's loyal friend, comforting him daily through life's ups and downs. Aaron was a mess.

Life began to change the day Aaron's granddaughter was born. Her birth triggered deep, unrecognizable feelings within him. When this perfect little creature was placed in his arms, he melted. His knees weakened, and his head felt light. With this baby in his arms, it took all he had to keep himself from falling to the ground and losing consciousness. This was Aaron's defining moment. This was the moment he decided to RECALCULATE ROUTE.

At the lowest point in his life, Aaron stumbled across **"Vol 1—*one little thing*: how to make big leaps with tiny steps."** Feeling despair, he started reading the book. This brought him newfound hope. Aaron naturally identified himself as a Hare, because when he sets his mind to something, he gets it done quickly. Aaron wanted instant results, so he decided to read "**one little thing**" as a Hare, not as a Tortoise, as it was intended. He felt impatient. As he recalculated his route, he changed the basics in his life all at once instead of adding **one little thing** every four months. The results were astounding.

The first thing Aaron did was to let go of a toxic relationship that was causing more stress than he was willing to have anymore. After becoming emotionally free, he made a commitment to taking whole food concentrate capsules and two plant-based healthy smoothies every day no matter what. He drank enough water to keep his urine clear. Over time, he naturally lost the urge to drink the same amount of alcohol and felt compelled to eat a diet rich in fruits and vegetables. Aaron's attitude transformed in the process. He went from depressive and self-destructive to genuinely happy and grateful most of the time. Aaron also added a routine of walking and core strengthening to his days.

Within six months of his defining moment with his newborn granddaughter, Aaron let go of 10 inches of belly fat and forty nine pounds of scale weight. His alcohol consumption had dropped by two-thirds of what it was before his transformation. He continues to stay consistent with his lifestyle choices because he cannot imagine leaving his beautiful granddaughter on this earth to live her life without him. Today, Aaron's granddaughter is an important part of his life.

This chapter is for the Hare: the person who leaps forward and wants to do everything at once. I am a classic Hare. I understand the risks, the joys and the pitfalls of the Hare. I had three babies in forty one months. No twins. I understand *fast*!

Disclaimer to slower changing Turtles: you can skip this chapter. If you choose to read it, please don't feel pressured to take on more than you feel ready to do. The choice is always yours with every change.

To the Hares: the great transformation beckons you. Can you feel it?

You can do anything for thirty days.

The following process is NOT a diet. There is a three letter word in "die-t". I stay clear of this term simply because the general population has felt betrayed by the endless stream of diets over the past several decades. Why even go there? This is a cleanse.

Over a period of thirty days or longer, consider achieving this two-part process simultaneously: remove toxic chemicals from your fat cells and reduce the toxic load from the foods you are ingesting on a regular basis.

As I travel through life helping others to overhaul their engines, I notice a general anxiety in the average transformer. "How many things do I actually need to give up?" "How am I ever going to give up my wine...my coffee...my sweet bedtime treat...my_____?" Simply fill in the blank. Their answers always lie within their WHY, their reasons for starting in the first place. This is how they eventually get through it.

Make it fun. Do this with a buddy. Find your support tribe. Put boundaries up in front of people who are sabotaging you. You know who these people are. They criticize your efforts. They tempt you with foods and habits you know are toxic.

TRY THIS:

Overhaul your engine and change your filter.

The following health habits will overhaul your engine and change your filter by removing toxins from your body when practiced consistently over time.

Sleep for eight hours every night.

Turn off your mind chatter with deep breathing for at least five minutes every day.

Drink enough water to keep your urine clear all day.

Move your body as much as you can to get your blood pumping.

Add whole food concentrates to your day.

Drink two plant-based, protein smoothies, each with no more than 20 Grams of protein every day to offset wasteful calories and to pack in extra nutrition.

Do not eat anything after 7:00 pm to rest your digestion at night.

Eat only clean foods with certified organic or GMO-free ingredients.

Remove all gluten, dairy, alcohol, caffeine, added sugar, and processed health-depleting foods from your food choices. No need to remove meat and fish, but the idea is to remove toxins from your food supply. Choose to eat clean, organic grass fed meat and wild fish.

Never go more than three hours without eating something since you will want to keep your blood sugar steady and stable throughout the day. I keep high quality protein bars with me at all times in case I can't find something clean to eat around me.

A typical blended smoothie will have a milk alternative or coconut water base, green leafy vegetables, ground organic flax seeds, soaked chia seeds, fruit, and plant protein powder. Try to resist the temptation to include animal products in your smoothie, such as cow's milk, whey protein or yogurt. Animal protein has been proven to cause general inflammation and may deliver unwanted toxicity into the body.

This is NOT about transforming you into a vegan. This is NOT about depriving you of calories. This is NOT about suppressing your appetite. This IS about doing what it takes to meet your health goals in a fast-paced world. This IS about reaching a higher place in your development. This IS about having energy and feeling better about yourself and your life, so you can get stuff done and have more fun.

Healthy snacks include: Hummus, avocados, cherry tomatoes, organic edamame beans, fresh fruit, celery sticks, nut butter without hydrogenated or partially hydrogenated oil, hard boiled eggs, organic popcorn, carrots, clean trail mix, apples, sweet potatoes, fresh salsa and guacamole.

A typical day in the life of a transformer:

0600 – Some form of cardiovascular movement, stretching, or core strengthening

0700 – Blended Smoothie

1000 – Mid morning healthy snack

1200 – Clean, plant-based lunch

1500 – Smoothie or healthy snack

1830 – Smoothie or light dinner

2200 – Get some sleep

That's the plan for Hares who want to create fast transformation. Feel free to try all of it, or whatever parts feel right to you now. Or don't. The choice is yours.

CHAPTER SIX

Lightening J-O-L-T

The JOLT

Choosing *one little thing* to improve your life is a journey. When you decide what your *one little thing* is, please don't feel like it is etched in stone and handed down to Moses. Try looking at your journey as a trail of infinite choices simply floating in space. Choices are based on either education or trial and error. They could be based on both. Your choices should remain interchangeable and flexible.

Don't be afraid to fail your way to success.

It may take fourteen failures to create the kind of success that makes the difference for you. If *one little thing* doesn't work for you, try another *one little thing*. It doesn't mean that you have failed or that you are a failure. It simply means that you are RECALCULATING ROUTE and taking one step closer to success. The "failures" are what cause you to feel emotional anguish, but those same failures will eventually allow you to feel accomplished and successful. They are all part of your journey.

You WILL relapse at times.

You WILL become frustrated by not staying on course.

You WILL feel like beating yourself up at some point along the way.

Before you repudiate yourself to the land of the lost losers once again, consider an alternative way of experiencing your disgust.

Unfortunately, this self-loathing behavior is normal and quite common during the process of making positive changes to your health. If you don't feel this way from time to time, congratulations. You ARE the exception.

As you begin your journey into the dark side, it is important, to identify how you feel. This step is an important part of your self-discovery. You don't necessarily have to do anything with these feelings. Simply identify them. Are you feeling sad? Are you feeling angry? Are you experiencing shame, apathy, or desperation? Own the feeling. Don't worry about doing anything with it…just own it for now.

This is a good time to define some of the self-loathing language. Come on, you're thinking it anyway. Allow me to help you through this step. Simply fill in the blanks with your name and you will be on your way to self-discovery.

"I am the biggest loser on the planet."

"I can never complete anything."

"Why do I continually put myself through this torture?"

"I should have never started doing this. I knew I wouldn't be able to do this."

"What a loser."

"Really…?"

"What kind of example am I setting for my kids who are watching me?"

"My wife thinks I'm a loser too."

Go to the dark side and stay there for as long as you like…a day, a week, a year if you need to do so.

Now that you are fully present on the dark side of your self-destructive process, it might be helpful to write down the phrase that you like to use. You know what it is:_____

_____

DO NOT SKIP THIS STEP. It is critical to your process. Go back to the blank space now and put your own words on the page. Be in control of your own flogging.

Time has passed. Was it an hour? Was it a day, a week or a year?

Who cares?

Let's move on. If you are feeling as though the storm has passed and you are feeling somewhat emotionally drained, you might be ready to move forward and take the next three steps.

STEP 1: Create your defining moment for RECALCULATING ROUTE. Decide that it is time.

STEP 2: Go back to chapter one and identify the reason WHY you decided it was time to make changes in the first place. Be sure to connect with the emotion behind your WHY.

Has your WHY changed between the time you started reading the book and now? If you put deep thought into that initial step in chapter one, a drastic change in your WHY is unlikely. If it has changed, re-write your WHY and bookmark the page for quick reference when you start beating yourself up again.

J-O-L-T is an acronym for *just-one-little-thing*. This is a book about doing only one thing at a time in order to achieve successful results.

Step 3: Go back to your ***one little thing***.

GET BACK ON THE HIGHWAY AND KEEP GOING!

References

1. Loftus CG, Loftus EV, Jr., Harmsen WS, et al. Update on the incidence and prevalence of Crohn's disease and ulcerative colitis in Olmsted County, Minnesota, 1940-2000. Inflamm Bowel Dis. 2007;13:254-261.

2. Herrinton LF, Liu L, Lewis JD, Griffin PM, Allison J. Incidence and prevalence of inflammatory bowel disease in a Northern California managed-care organization, 1996-2002. Am J Gastroenterol. 2008;103(8):1998-2006.

3. Center for Disease Control, June 2010; National Center for Health Statistics. Source: Prevalence of Overweight, Obesity, and Extreme obesity Among Adults, United States, Trends 1960-1962 through 2007-2008 by Cynthia L. Ogden, Ph.D., and Margaret D. Carroll, S.S.P.H., Division of health and Nutrition Examination Surveys.

4. Center for Disease control, December 2010; National Center for Health statistics, Vital Health Stat 10(249), 2010. Source: Summary health Statistics for U.S. Adults: National health Interview Survey, 2009. By Pleis JR, Ward BW, Lucas JW.

5. CDC, NCHS. Underlying Cause of Death 1999-2013 on CDC WONDER Online Database, released 2015. Data are from the Multiple Cause of Death Files, 1999-2013, as compiled from data provided by the 57 vital statistics jurisdictions through the Vital Statistics Cooperative Program. Accessed Feb. 3, 2015.

6. Center for Disease control, December 2010; National Center for Health statistics, Vital Health Stat 10(249), 2010. Source: Summary health Statistics for U.S. Adults: National health Interview Survey, 2009. By Pleis JR, Ward BW, Lucas JW.

7. *The Relaxation Response*, 1975; Herbert Benson, Harvard physician, and Miriam Z. Klipper. The Response is a simple version of Transcendental Meditation (TM) presented for people in the Western world.

8. National Institute of Health; Alterations in Intestinal Permeability. MC Arrieta, L Bistritz and J B Meddings. Article: http://www.ncbi.nlm.nih.gov/pmc/articles/PMC1856434/

9. The Food & Chemical Toxicology Journal, University of Caen, September 2012, Gilles-Eric Seralini; "A Comparison of the Effects of Three GM Corn Varieties on Mammalian Health", http://www.biolsci.org/v05p0706.htm

10. Carotene and Retinol Efficacy Trial (CARET study), performed by researchers at Fred Hutchisnson Cancer Research Center in Seattle, WA. http://www.compass.fhcrc.org/caretweb/

11. http://www.JuicePlus.com

25093092R00063

Made in the USA
Columbia, SC
01 September 2018